Earn Loyalty, Not Respect

by Dwayne Farr

The Power of Loyalty

The Power of Loyalty

Loyalty is a remarkable force that can shape and strengthen relationships in both personal and professional settings. It is a testament to the trust, respect, and genuine connection between individuals. In today's fast-paced and ever-changing world, building and maintaining loyalty has become increasingly valuable.

Loyalty has the power to transform businesses and organizations. When employees are loyal to their company, they display dedication and commitment to its success. They go above and beyond their duties, taking initiative and investing their time and energy to contribute to the growth and prosperity of the organization. Their loyalty creates a positive work culture, inspiring their colleagues to align with the company's goals and values. This collective loyalty fosters teamwork, cooperation, and innovation, ultimately leading to greater productivity and success.

Moreover, loyalty from clients and customers is vital for the growth and sustainability of any business. When customers are loyal to a brand, they remain devoted despite competition or changing market dynamics. They choose to repeatedly engage with the brand, purchase their products or services, and advocate for the company to others. Their loyalty is not merely transactional, but deeply rooted in their belief in the brand's quality, reliability, and values. This unwavering support from loyal customers creates a strong foundation for business growth, as it reduces the need for costly marketing efforts and builds a loyal customer base that consistently generates revenue.

Loyalty in personal relationships is equally significant. It creates a sense of security and stability, allowing individuals to rely on one another during times of need. In romantic partnerships, loyalty forms the bedrock of trust, faithfulness, and commitment. It enables couples to navigate challenges and conflicts with resilience and compassion, knowing that they have each other's backs through thick and thin. Likewise, in friendships, loyalty builds a sense of camaraderie and companionship. Friends who are loyal support and uplift one another, sharing joyful moments and providing solace during difficult times. The power of loyal friendships lies in the understanding that someone is there for you, unconditionally.

Loyalty is deeply rooted in human nature. From the earliest stages of human history, loyalty played a significant role in survival and social cohesion. Our ancestors formed tribes and relied on the loyalty within these groups to protect themselves from external threats. Loyalty was an essential mechanism for survival, as individuals who were loyal to the group were more likely to receive support and protection when needed. This innate human instinct for loyalty continues to influence our actions and relationships today. People tend to seek out loyalty in their personal and professional lives because it provides a sense of belonging and safety, allowing them to navigate the complexities of life with greater confidence and support.

The power of loyalty lies in its ability to create a sense of belonging and trust. When individuals are loyal to one another, they build strong bonds that surpass superficial connections. Loyalty acts as a glue that holds relationships together during challenging times. It fosters a deep understanding and appreciation for one another, giving each person the assurance that they can rely on each other unconditionally.

Moreover, loyalty breeds reciprocity. When one person displays loyalty to another, it often encourages the other person to reciprocate. This reciprocity creates a positive cycle where both parties strive to support and uplift each other, further deepening the bond between them. The mutual trust and commitment formed through loyalty lay the foundation for successful collaborations and partnerships.

So, how can one harness the power of loyalty? It starts with understanding that loyalty is a two-way street. To earn loyalty, you must first be loyal to others. This means being reliable, keeping your promises, and consistently delivering on your commitments. It involves being present and attentive to the needs of others, whether it be a friend, a colleague, or a customer. By consistently demonstrating loyalty, you build a reputation for trustworthiness and dependability, making it more likely for others to reciprocate.

Additionally, loyalty is built through genuine care and empathy. It's about understanding the needs and concerns of others and providing support when they need it. It requires active listening and showing a genuine interest in people's lives and aspirations. By being empathetic, you create a safe space for others to express themselves openly, and that fosters a sense of trust and loyalty.

Transparency and open communication are also crucial in building loyalty. Sharing information and being honest, even when the news may be difficult, fosters trust. People appreciate transparency, and it strengthens the bond between individuals. When there is open communication, misunderstandings and conflicts can be resolved quickly, allowing the relationship to grow stronger.

Furthermore, loyalty thrives in an environment that fosters personal growth and development. When individuals feel supported in their aspirations and provided with opportunities to learn and advance, they are more likely to remain loyal. Encouraging and recognizing their achievements, and providing mentorship and guidance, builds trust and loyalty. When individuals believe that their personal and professional growth is valued and nurtured, they are more likely to remain loyal to the organization.

Lastly, fostering a sense of community and belonging is essential in cultivating loyalty. When individuals feel valued and included, they are more likely to stay committed and loyal. Building a supportive and inclusive environment encourages individuals to invest their time and energy in the relationship. By creating a sense of belonging, you make others feel like they are an integral part of something greater, and that strengthens their loyalty.

In conclusion, the power of loyalty lies in its ability to strengthen connections, create trust, and foster a sense of belonging. Loyalty is not merely a transactional exchange; it is a deep and meaningful connection between individuals. By understanding the importance of loyalty and consistently demonstrating it to others, we can harness this powerful force and create lasting relationships that contribute to personal and professional success. The innate human instinct for loyalty, coupled with genuine care, transparency, a focus on personal growth, and a sense of community, allows us to tap into the true power of loyalty and experience its transformative effects.

The Difference Between Loyalty and Respect

Loyalty and respect are often used interchangeably, but they are distinct concepts that play different roles in relationships. While both are important, understanding the difference between loyalty and respect can help us navigate our interactions with others more effectively.

Respect is the foundation of any healthy relationship, whether it be personal or professional. It is a fundamental aspect of treating others with dignity and acknowledging their inherent worth. When we respect someone, we not only value their thoughts and perspectives, but we also recognize their boundaries and rights. Respect allows us to create an atmosphere of trust and open communication, where individuals feel heard and understood.

Respecting others involves actively listening to their opinions, even if we may disagree with them. It means refraining from judgment and taking the time to understand their experiences and viewpoints. By recognizing and appreciating the uniqueness of each individual, we cultivate a more inclusive and compassionate environment.

In a personal context, respect is the cornerstone of healthy relationships, be it between friends, romantic partners, or family members. It encompasses treating others with kindness, empathy, and consideration. Respectful communication involves expressing oneself assertively yet constructively, while also respecting the autonomy and feelings of the other person. By embracing respect, we create an environment where individuals feel valued and empowered, leading to deeper connections and greater well-being.

In professional settings, respect is crucial for maintaining a positive work environment, fostering collaboration, and valuing diverse perspectives. Employees can respect their superiors and colleagues by treating them with dignity, listening actively, and valuing their contributions. Respect cultivates an atmosphere where ideas can be freely exchanged, and conflicts can be resolved constructively. It also enables individuals to feel psychologically safe, encouraging them to share their perspectives openly and contribute their unique talents to the organization's success.

However, respect alone may not be enough to sustain relationships in the long term. This is where loyalty comes into play – it goes beyond respect by encompassing a deep sense of commitment and dedication to a person, idea, or cause. Loyalty is demonstrated through unwavering support, trust, and reliability. It means standing by someone, not just in times of success and happiness, but also during difficult times or when faced with opposing opinions.

This steadfast devotion is forged through shared experiences, trust, and a mutual understanding of each other's values and goals. Loyalty often stems from a sense of gratitude, reciprocation, or a belief in a common purpose. It is a pledge to support and uplift the person or cause, even when faced with challenges or temptations to do otherwise.

However, loyalty is a complex concept that can be influenced by various factors. Blind loyalty can be dangerous, leading to enabling destructive behaviors or following without question. Therefore, loyalty must always be accompanied by respect, integrity, and a commitment to ethical conduct. It requires critical thinking and the ability to discern when loyalty is warranted and when it conflicts with one's values. Genuine loyalty is grounded in a shared vision, core values, and ethical principles.

In personal relationships, loyalty often builds over time, as people gradually earn each other's trust and demonstrate consistent support and reliability. It involves being there for someone in both good times and bad, providing a sense of security and dependability. Loyalty fosters deep connections and an emotional bond, strengthening the foundation of the relationship.

Similarly, in professional settings, loyalty takes on a different dimension. While employees are expected to be loyal to their organizations and adhere to its values, loyalty to individuals may fluctuate based on the quality of relationships and experiences. Loyalty should be earned through consistent leadership, timely recognition, and fair treatment. Trust plays a pivotal role in building and maintaining loyalty within professional relationships.

Loyalty is a reciprocal exchange. Leaders and organizations must also demonstrate loyalty to their employees by providing a safe and inclusive work environment, respecting their rights, and acknowledging their contributions. This reciprocal loyalty fosters a sense of belonging, encourages personal growth, and boosts overall job satisfaction.

In conclusion, understanding the difference between loyalty and respect is vital for nurturing healthy relationships. While respect is the foundation upon which all relationships should be built, loyalty is the commitment to support and stand by someone or something. By cultivating respect and earning loyalty, we create an environment where trust, collaboration, and personal growth can thrive. It is essential to strike a balance, recognizing when loyalty is warranted and when respect is sufficient, to ensure healthy and mutually beneficial connections.

Building Trust: The Key to Lasting Loyalty

Building Trust: The Key to Lasting Loyalty

Trust is the cornerstone of any successful and enduring relationship. In the context of loyalty, trust takes on even greater importance as it becomes the bedrock upon which loyalty is built. Without trust, loyalty remains fragile and easily broken. It is through the conscious cultivation of trust that we can develop and sustain strong and lasting connections.

Transparency and honesty play crucial roles in establishing trust. Transparency involves being open and forthcoming in our communications, sharing information openly, and willingly. When we are transparent, we signal to others that we have nothing to hide and that we respect their right to know. It creates an atmosphere of trust where individuals feel safe and secure and are more likely to share their thoughts, concerns, and aspirations. Transparency requires not only sharing information with others but also being honest with ourselves. It means having the courage to examine our own beliefs, motivations, and limitations, and aligning our actions with our values and principles.

In addition to transparency, trust is fortified through consistency and reliability. People are more likely to trust those who consistently demonstrate integrity and deliver on their promises. Consistency is about showing up consistently, whether it be in meeting deadlines, following through on commitments, or holding true to our values. When others see that our actions align with our words, it establishes a level of predictability and reliability that fosters trust. Reliability is about being someone others can depend on when they need support or assistance. By consistently meeting our obligations, being available when needed, and offering a helping hand, we establish a track record of dependability, building trust in the process.

Active listening and empathy are essential in building trust. Trust flourishes when others feel genuinely heard and understood. Active listening involves giving our undivided attention, suspending judgment, and seeking to understand before being understood. It requires us to be fully present and engaged in the conversation, showing respect for others' perspectives and experiences. By actively listening, we validate the importance of their voice and create an environment where trust can take root. Empathy goes hand in hand with active listening, as it allows us to put ourselves in others' shoes and genuinely connect with their emotions and needs. When we demonstrate genuine care and understanding, it deepens the trust in our relationships, creating a strong and lasting bond.

Consistency between our words and actions also plays a vital role in building trust. Integrity and authenticity are critical components of trust-building. When there are inconsistencies between what we say and what we do, it sows seeds of doubt and erodes trust. People need to see that our actions align consistently with our professed values and principles. When there is harmony between our words and behaviors, it generates confidence in our character and promotes trust in our intentions. Continuously striving to bridge the gap between our intentions and actions builds a foundation of trust that sustains and strengthens our relationships.

Forgiveness and the willingness to give others the benefit of the doubt further contribute to trust-building. We all make mistakes; it is a part of our human nature. However, when we exhibit forgiveness and understanding towards others' errors or lapses, we demonstrate compassion and care. Forgiveness allows us to rebuild trust after it has been broken, as it gives others the opportunity to learn from their mistakes and grow. When we trust others to make amends and extend forgiveness, we reinforce the health and resilience of our relationships. By nurturing an environment where forgiveness is valued, we create a space for trust to flourish and loyalty to deepen.

In summary, cultivating trust is essential for fostering lasting loyalty. It necessitates transparency, consistency, active listening, authenticity, and forgiveness. Trust creates a firm foundation upon which loyalty can thrive, enabling individuals and organizations to build resilient and meaningful connections. By prioritizing trust in our relationships, we pave the way for mutual understanding, support, and growth, enhancing our personal and professional lives. It is through trust that we can unlock the true power of loyalty, creating a bond that withstands the tests of time.

Integrity: The Bedrock of Loyalty

Integrity: The Bedrock of Loyalty

Integrity is a fundamental pillar of loyalty, serving as the compass that guides our actions and shapes our character. Rooted in honesty, authenticity, and moral fortitude, integrity is the cornerstone upon which trust and credibility are built. It is the unwavering commitment to doing what is right, even when faced with challenges or temptations.

At the very essence of integrity lies the alignment of our thoughts, words, and deeds. It is the living embodiment of our values and beliefs, transcending superficiality and forming an unbreakable bond between our inner moral compass and our outward behavior. When integrity permeates our lives, our relationships are fortified by a deep sense of trust and reliability.

Integrity in loyalty extends far beyond mere promises and commitments. It is a holistic approach to life that influences our interactions with others. When we operate with integrity, we place the needs and well-being of others at the forefront, consistently acting in their best interests. This genuine concern for others' welfare creates a sense of security and respect, nurturing loyalty in our personal and professional relationships.

In business, integrity cultivates a culture of trust, transparency, and ethical conduct. Customers seek out brands that consistently demonstrate integrity, knowing that they can rely on the quality and value of their products or services. Employees, too, are drawn to organizations that prioritize integrity, fostering an environment of fairness, honesty, and open communication. This mutual trust between employers, employees, and customers fosters loyalty and dedication, leading to increased productivity, customer retention, and overall success.

Maintaining integrity requires ongoing self-reflection, as we continuously evaluate our actions against our core values and principles. This introspection allows us to identify areas of growth and improvement, as well as the need to make amends for past mistakes. True integrity is not about perfection but rather the willingness to take ownership of our missteps and learn from them. By embracing personal accountability, we demonstrate resilience and a commitment to personal growth.

Integrity, at its core, is a manifestation of moral courage. It empowers us to stand firmly in our convictions, even in the face of opposition or adversity. This moral courage enables us to make difficult choices guided by our principles, rather than succumbing to the pressures of expediency or personal gain. When we choose integrity over convenience, we inspire others to do the same, fostering a collective commitment to honesty and ethics.

The importance of integrity extends beyond individual relationships and business transactions. It is the bedrock on which a just and equitable society is built. A society that values integrity values transparency, truth, and fairness. It acknowledges the importance of mutual respect and ethical conduct, creating an environment that fosters cooperation and unity. In such a society, integrity forms the backbone of institutions and systems, ensuring that they serve the common good rather than personal interests.

Ultimately, embodying integrity is a continuous journey, one that requires discipline and self-awareness. It calls us to be vigilant in examining our motives and choices, always striving for alignment between our values and actions. This unwavering commitment to integrity inspires loyalty in others, as they witness the sincere and consistent way in which we conduct ourselves.

Let us embrace integrity as a guiding principle in all aspects of our lives. By doing so, we contribute to the growth and development of ourselves, our relationships, our organizations, and society as a whole. Integrity, indeed, is the bedrock upon which loyalty thrives, illuminating our path towards a more prosperous and harmonious world.

Authenticity: Being Genuine in Your Interactions

Authenticity: Being Genuine in Your Interactions

In today's fast-paced and often superficial world, where social media platforms encourage the creation of curated personas and celebrities are manufactured overnight, authenticity has become a rare gem. It is the quality that sets individuals apart, allows them to build genuine connections, and establishes a sense of trust and loyalty. As a writer, your ability to explore and embrace your authenticity is paramount in creating a unique voice that resonates with readers. In this chapter, we will delve even deeper into the importance of being authentic in your interactions, and how it can contribute to building lasting connections with your readership.

Being authentic is not a skill that can be learned overnight. It is a continuous journey of self-discovery and self-acceptance. To be truly authentic, you need to be honest with yourself and others about your thoughts, feelings, and values. It requires self-awareness and the courage to be vulnerable, revealing your true self to the world. Authenticity is not about putting on a mask or trying to fit into a particular mold. It is about embracing your strengths and flaws, and being comfortable with who you genuinely are.

Inauthenticity, on the other hand, can be felt by others like a false note in a symphony. It creates a sense of disconnect and erodes trust. When you are authentic, you allow your true essence to shine through your words, attracting readers who resonate with your genuine expression. Your authenticity becomes a beacon, enlightening and inspiring others who share your values or have similar experiences.

When you approach your writing with authenticity, the reader can sense your sincerity. Your words carry more weight because they come from a place of truth and genuine expression. Authenticity in writing means conveying your ideas, experiences, and emotions with honesty, even if they may be difficult or challenging to share. It is about stepping out of your comfort zone and revealing the depths of your soul. By doing this, you allow your readers to connect with your work on a deeper level and establish a meaningful bond. They recognize the value of your authenticity and appreciate the rawness and realness you offer.

Authenticity also creates a sense of relatability. When readers encounter a writer who is unapologetically genuine, they feel a connection to the author's story. They see themselves reflected in the pages, finding comfort and understanding in knowing that they are not alone in their experiences. This connection fosters a sense of trust and loyalty, as readers come to rely on your authentic voice to provide them with insightful and relatable content. Your authenticity gives them permission to explore their own truths and embrace their uniqueness, creating a more inclusive and empathetic space.

To be authentic in your interactions, it is crucial to be self-aware and mindful. Take the time to reflect on your values, beliefs, and strengths. Understand what makes you unique and embrace it wholeheartedly. Let your writing reflect your true self. Avoid the temptation to imitate others or conform to societal expectations. Celebrate your individuality and share it with the world, for it is in embracing your authentic voice that you will find your own distinctive style and leave a lasting impact on your readers.

Authenticity also means being honest about your limitations and mistakes. As a writer, you are bound to encounter challenges or make errors. Instead of hiding or covering them up, acknowledge them openly. Admitting your mistakes and sharing the lessons you've learned showcases your authenticity and vulnerability. It humanizes you and makes you more relatable to your readers. It demonstrates that you too are a work in progress and that growth and learning are an integral part of your journey as a writer. Your transparency not only strengthens your credibility but also teaches your readers that failure and setbacks are stepping stones to success.

In conclusion, authenticity is a powerful tool that writers can harness to build loyalty and trust among their readers. By embracing your true self, expressing your thoughts and feelings sincerely, and sharing your strengths and vulnerabilities, you can create genuine connections. Let your authenticity shine through in your writing, and watch as readers gravitate towards your genuine voice. Remember, being authentic is not only about gaining readership, it is about staying true to yourself as a famous writer—a writer who leaves an indelible mark by being genuine in every interaction. Embrace your authenticity and let it guide your path to profound connection and meaningful impact.

Empathy: Understanding and Connecting with Others

Empathy: Understanding and Connecting with Others

In a world driven by technology and fast-paced interactions, empathy often takes a back seat. However, as we strive to build and maintain loyal relationships, empathy becomes an essential element in our journey. It is the key to unlocking meaningful connections and fostering understanding in an increasingly disconnected world.

Empathy is the ability to truly understand and share the feelings of others. It is not merely sympathy, which is acknowledging someone's emotions from a distance. Empathy requires actively immersing ourselves in someone else's shoes, feeling what they feel, and responding with genuine compassion and understanding.

But what exactly enables us to be empathetic? How can we develop this skill and use it to deepen our connections with others? The foundations of empathy lie in presence, active listening, suspension of judgment, validation, appreciation for diversity, and taking action.

Presence is the cornerstone of empathy. In our hyperconnected lives, it is essential to set aside distractions and be fully engaged in our interactions. By doing so, we create a space that allows us to truly connect with others. When we give our undivided attention, we not only pick up on verbal cues but also nonverbal ones that reveal underlying emotions. A comforting touch, a furrowed brow, or a trembling voice can speak volumes about what someone is experiencing. By being fully present, we show respect and genuine interest in understanding the emotions of others.

Active listening is paramount in empathy. It requires us to not just hear words but truly understand the emotions behind them. This involves focusing on the speaker's message, seeking clarification when needed, and acknowledging the deeper emotions hidden beneath their words. When we listen with empathy, we create a safe and non-judgmental space in which individuals can express themselves freely.

To cultivate empathy, we must also suspend judgment. As human beings, we often bring our own biases and preconceived notions into our interactions. These internal filters can hinder our ability to truly understand others. By consciously setting aside our judgments and approaching each interaction with an open mind, we create space for genuine connection.

Diverse perspectives and experiences enrich our understanding of the world and amplify our capacity for empathy.

Validation is another vital aspect of empathy. When someone shares their emotions or experiences, they seek reassurance that their feelings are valid and respected. We can provide this validation by acknowledging their emotions and expressing empathy towards their situation. Validating another person's emotions does not require us to agree with their perspective; rather, it means recognizing the legitimacy of their feelings and conveying our understanding and support.

Furthermore, empathy extends beyond understanding emotions alone. It encompasses recognizing and appreciating the unique experiences and perspectives of others. To truly connect with others, we must actively seek to understand different cultures, backgrounds, and viewpoints. By embracing diversity, we broaden our empathy and strengthen our connections with a wider range of individuals. Learning about the customs, traditions, and histories of others fosters appreciation, acceptance, and a deeper understanding of their journeys.

However, empathy is not limited to understanding alone. It calls us to take action. True empathy means actively supporting and helping others when needed. It means going beyond merely feeling and understanding their emotions, but also providing comfort, assistance, and encouragement. Taking action demonstrates our commitment to building loyal relationships and solidifies the trust we have developed through empathy.

In summary, empathy is a powerful tool in building and sustaining loyalty. By seeking to understand, connecting with others on an emotional level, suspending judgment, validating their experiences, embracing diversity, and taking action, we can forge deep and meaningful connections. Cultivating empathy not only benefits others but also enriches our own lives by fostering mutual understanding and trust. So, let us strive to be empathetic in our interactions and reap the rewards of profound and lasting loyalty.

Consistency: The Secret to Sustaining Loyalty

Consistency: The Secret to Sustaining Loyalty

In the journey towards earning and sustaining loyalty, consistency plays a pivotal role. Consistency is the key that unlocks the door to trust, reliability, and dependability. When individuals and organizations consistently deliver on their promises and maintain their principles over time, they garner respect and admiration from those around them.

Consistency is not a one-time act; it is a behavior that must be embedded in one's character and actions. It requires a deep understanding of one's values, beliefs, and priorities. By knowing oneself and what one stands for, individuals can uphold consistency in all aspects of their lives.

To establish consistency, it is crucial to set clear expectations from the beginning. Clearly communicate your values, goals, and standards to those you interact with. By setting these expectations, you are paving the way for consistency in your behaviors and decisions. It also allows others to align their expectations with yours, creating harmony and understanding.

Consistency requires discipline and self-awareness. It means following through on your commitments, even when it may be challenging or inconvenient. It means staying true to your values and principles, even when faced with temptations or external pressures. Consistency demands integrity, as it requires aligning your actions with your words consistently.

Inconsistency can erode trust and damage relationships. When people experience inconsistency from others, they may become hesitant to rely on them. Inconsistency creates uncertainty and confusion, undermining the foundation of loyalty that has been built. It is essential to be aware of your actions and their impact on others to avoid such pitfalls.

Consistency is not about being static or stagnant. It is about being adaptable while still maintaining your core values and principles. Consistency does not mean never changing but rather adapting and evolving in a way that is true to your character. Being consistent in one's growth and development shows others a willingness to learn and improve, which further strengthens loyalty.

Consistency is a continuous process. It requires ongoing effort and attention to maintain over time. It may be tempting to let consistency slip when faced with challenges or obstacles, but this is when it is most crucial to remain steadfast. Consistency in the face of adversity demonstrates resilience and determination, earning even greater respect and loyalty.

Sustaining loyalty through consistency requires self-reflection and self-accountability. Regularly evaluate your actions, ensuring they align with your values and goals. Seek feedback from those around you to gauge how your consistency is being perceived. With this self-awareness, you can make adjustments and course corrections along the way, deepening the loyalty you have already earned.

In addition to personal consistency, consistency within organizations is equally important in sustaining loyalty. Organizations that consistently deliver quality products or services build a reputation for reliability. By providing a consistent experience, they create a sense of trust and dependability, which encourages loyalty in their customers.

Consistency also extends to communication. When organizations consistently communicate their messages with clarity and transparency, customers and stakeholders feel informed and included. Consistent communication builds trust and loyalty by reducing uncertainty and creating a sense of connection.

Another facet of consistency lies in the consistency of policies and procedures. When organizations consistently implement and enforce fair and just policies, they foster an environment of trust and employee loyalty. Likewise, consistency in decision-making and adhering to ethical standards reinforces an organization's integrity and commitment to their values.

Consistency should also be applied in leadership. Leaders who exemplify consistency in their actions and decisions inspire loyalty and trust among their followers. When leaders consistently uphold their values, honor their commitments, and treat others with fairness and respect, they create a culture of loyalty, dedication, and motivation within their teams.

Furthermore, consistency is closely tied to reputation. Individuals and organizations that consistently deliver on their promises and maintain high standards develop a positive reputation that precedes them. A consistent track record earns the trust of potential clients, customers, and partners, making it easier to attract new opportunities and build long-lasting relationships. A good reputation becomes a valuable asset that requires ongoing consistency to uphold and enhance.

Moreover, consistency not only applies to actions and decisions, but it also extends to emotional consistency. People are drawn to and feel more secure around individuals who consistently display emotional stability. When others can rely on your consistent emotional responses, they feel a sense of comfort and confidence in their interactions with you.

Consistency thrives in an environment of accountability. Holding oneself accountable for maintaining consistency is essential, but so is fostering accountability among team members and stakeholders. By establishing clear expectations, setting goals, and regularly evaluating progress, individuals and organizations can cultivate a culture of shared accountability, further strengthening loyalty.

Consistency is not without its challenges. It requires discipline, resilience, and self-reflection. There will be times when maintaining consistency seems difficult or when the temptation to deviate presents itself. However, it is during these moments that the true power of consistency is revealed, as it demonstrates the strength of character and unwavering commitment.

In conclusion, consistency is the secret ingredient to sustaining loyalty. By consistently demonstrating your commitment, reliability, and integrity, you can earn and maintain the trust and loyalty of others. Remember, it takes time and effort to build loyalty, but with consistency as your guiding principle, you will create lasting relationships that stand the test of time. Consistency is not just an occasional action but a way of life that fosters trust, reliability, and enduring loyalty.

Nurturing Relationships: A Blueprint for Loyalty

Nurturing Relationships: A Blueprint for Loyalty

In the quest to build and maintain loyalty, nurturing relationships is an essential aspect that cannot be overlooked. Like any relationship, professional connections need care and attention to flourish. Just as you would water a plant or tend to a garden, investing in relationships is crucial for long-term success.

First and foremost, it is essential to establish a solid foundation based on trust and mutual respect. Trust goes beyond mere reliability; it encompasses integrity, transparency, and consistent behavior. By aligning your actions with your words and consistently demonstrating your dependability, you lay the groundwork for trust to flourish. Building trust requires time and effort, but it is a fundamental pillar that cannot be compromised.

Moreover, trust alone is not enough; respect is equally vital in nurturing relationships. Respect implies valuing the opinions, perspectives, and boundaries of others. It means treating others with professionalism and kindness, even in the face of disagreement. Genuine respect fosters a sense of safety, creating an environment where individuals feel comfortable expressing themselves openly and honestly. By embracing diversity and appreciating the unique strengths and experiences of each person, you can cultivate an inclusive and respectful atmosphere that nurtures loyalty.

In building trust and respect, effective communication plays a pivotal role. Clear and open lines of communication establish a shared understanding and foster deeper connections. Actively listen to others, seeking to understand their viewpoints rather than simply waiting for your turn to speak. Engage in meaningful conversations, acknowledging and validating their thoughts and feelings. Avoid interrupting or dismissing their perspectives, as it can erode trust and hinder the growth of loyalty. By practicing active and empathetic listening, you demonstrate your commitment to understanding others and building strong relationships.

Furthermore, it is crucial to take a genuine interest in the lives and aspirations of those whom you seek to build loyalty with. People want to feel seen and heard, both in their personal and professional lives. By showing authentic curiosity and investing time to understand their goals, passions, and challenges, you can develop a deeper connection with them. Take note of their achievements, ask meaningful questions about their interests, and offer support and encouragement when they face obstacles. Demonstrating your investment in their success fosters a sense of loyalty, as individuals are more likely to reciprocate when they feel genuinely cared for.

Understanding the motivations and drivers of those around you is another vital component of nurturing relationships. Each person has unique aspirations and desires, and recognizing these individual motivations helps tailor your interactions to their specific needs. Some individuals may prioritize growth and development, while others place a higher value on work-life balance or recognition. By understanding these personal drivers, you can offer targeted guidance, resources, and support to help individuals achieve their goals. This customized approach shows that you truly care about their success and strengthens the bond of loyalty.

Consistency is a key factor in nurturing relationships. Be consistent in your words, actions, and availability. Reliability builds trust and confidence, assuring others that they can count on you in times of need. Follow through on your commitments and meet deadlines consistently, as missed expectations can damage trust and strain relationships. Consistency also extends to your behavior and demeanor. Maintain a positive attitude, even during challenging times, and treat everyone with fairness and kindness. Consistent actions and attitudes help establish your reputation as a reliable and trustworthy ally, further solidifying the foundation for loyalty.

Adaptability is another critical attribute in maintaining relationships. As individuals grow and evolve, their needs and expectations may change. Be open-minded and receptive to these shifts, adjusting your strategies and approaches accordingly. Flexibility allows for a more dynamic and responsive relationship, demonstrating your ability to adapt, grow, and support others through various circumstances. By showing a willingness to change and evolve with the needs of the relationship, you foster an environment of mutual growth and loyalty.

Moreover, it is essential to actively and generously support the success and well-being of those within your network. Offer assistance, resources, and advice when possible, even if it doesn't directly benefit you. Providing value and going above and beyond creates a sense of reciprocity and deepens the bond of loyalty. Celebrate the achievements of others openly and acknowledge their contributions, whether privately or publicly. By promoting a culture of appreciation and gratitude, you inspire loyalty among those around you.

However, it's important to note that loyalty is a two-way street. Just as you expect others to be loyal to you, be sure to reciprocate that loyalty. Stand by others during their difficulties. Be understanding and compassionate when they face setbacks, and provide support and solutions when needed. Loyalty requires empathy and understanding, as well as shared vulnerability and accountability. By demonstrating your unwavering support, you foster a sense of safety and loyalty that is reciprocated in return.

Lastly, it is crucial to continue nurturing relationships consistently. Regularly check in with the people you value and show genuine care for their well-being. Make an effort to stay connected, whether through face-to-face meetings, phone calls, or digital communication. Demonstrate your genuine interest in their lives by remembering important milestones and asking about their progress towards their goals. Continually invest in the relationship by sharing valuable resources, making meaningful introductions, or offering guidance and mentorship. By consistently showing up and being present, you reinforce the importance of the relationship and deepen the bond of loyalty.

Building and nurturing relationships is an ongoing process that requires dedication and investment. By prioritizing trust, respect, effective communication, genuine interest, understanding motivations, consistency, adaptability, support, and reciprocity, you can cultivate strong and enduring relationships. Remember, loyalty is not automatic; it is earned and cultivated over time. With genuine care and effort, you can create a blueprint for loyalty that brings mutual success and enriches both your personal and professional life.

Overcoming Challenges: Strengthening Loyalty in Difficult Times

In times of hardship and adversity, loyalty can be put to the ultimate test. It is during these difficult moments that true loyalty shines and proves its strength. However, maintaining loyalty in such challenging times requires extra effort, careful consideration, and a deep understanding of the dynamics at play.

The first step in overcoming challenges and strengthening loyalty is to acknowledge the difficult situation at hand. Whether it's a business setback, a personal crisis, or a global pandemic, it's important to openly address the challenges and communicate transparently with those involved. By acknowledging the gravity of the situation, you show your commitment to finding a solution and demonstrate your trustworthiness.

Transparent communication becomes even more crucial in times of difficulty. Not only should you share information, but you must also actively listen to the concerns and feedback of others. This includes both your colleagues, clients, or employees and those who may be indirectly impacted by the situation. Actively seek their opinions, take their perspectives into account, and address their questions and uncertainties. By fostering open dialogue, you create an environment of trust and strengthen the loyalty of those around you.

During challenging times, it's crucial to stay connected with your colleagues, clients, or employees. This can be done through regular check-ins, team meetings, or one-on-one conversations. By actively engaging and showing genuine concern, you convey that you value their loyalty and are committed to supporting them through the rough patch.

Empathy is also vital in times of difficulty. Put yourself in the shoes of those affected and try to understand their perspective. Recognize that everyone may be experiencing challenges in their personal lives, such as health issues, social isolation, or financial stress. By showing empathy, you build trust and strengthen the bond of loyalty. Offer your support and provide any necessary resources to help them navigate the challenges they face.

Transparency and honesty are non-negotiable when dealing with difficult times. Be open about any changes or decisions that may impact your colleagues, clients, or employees. Share information as soon as it becomes available to avoid any perceived lack of transparency. By maintaining open communication, you foster an environment of trust and loyalty.

Moreover, consider the long-term implications of your actions. How you handle challenges today will shape the loyalty you earn in the future. Take the opportunity to demonstrate your commitment and dedication to finding solutions, even if it means making tough decisions. Remember, loyalty is built upon a foundation of trust, and your actions during difficult times can either reinforce that trust or erode it.

In challenging times, it's essential to provide clear and purposeful leadership. Set realistic expectations while inspiring hope and resilience. This means actively assessing the situation, creating a strategy, and sharing it with your team. Be proactive in identifying potential obstacles and devise contingency plans to mitigate them. By demonstrating decisive leadership, you instill confidence in those around you, reinforcing their loyalty to your cause.

When facing adversity, it's vital to prioritize self-care and well-being. This not only applies to you but also to your colleagues, clients, or employees. Encourage and support mental health initiatives, promote a healthy work-life balance, and provide resources for self-care. By prioritizing well-being, you foster loyalty by showing genuine care and concern for the whole person, beyond just their professional contributions.

It's important to remember that loyalty is a two-way street. Just as you expect loyalty from others, you must also offer it in return. Show appreciation for the loyalty demonstrated by your colleagues, clients, or employees. Acknowledge their efforts, recognize their commitment, and reward their dedication. By nurturing a culture of reciprocity, you create an environment where loyalty flourishes.

Lastly, learn from the challenges you face. Reflect on what worked well and what could have been handled differently. Use these lessons to adapt and strengthen your approach in the future, ensuring that your relationships are fortified even in the face of adversity. Seek feedback from your colleagues, clients, or employees to understand their experiences and perspectives. Encourage open dialogue and continuously evolve your strategies based on the lessons learned.

Overcoming challenges and strengthening loyalty in difficult times requires resilience, empathy, decisive leadership, self-care, and a commitment to open, honest communication. By acknowledging and addressing the challenges head-on, staying connected, showing empathy, and prioritizing well-being, you can reinforce the loyalty you have worked tirelessly to build. Remember, difficult times are opportunities to demonstrate your true character and commitment to those who have placed their trust in you.